Contents

Words printed in **bold italic** are explained in the glossary.

What is paper?

Paper is one of the world's most useful materials. People use it every day. There are thousands of different kinds of paper, and these can be used to make all sorts of things.

Paper

by Claire Llewellyn

W
FRANKLIN WATTS
LONDON·SYDNEY

First published in 2001 by
Franklin Watts
96 Leonard Street
London EC2A 4XD

Franklin Watts Australia
56 O'Riordan Street
Alexandria
NSW 2015

Text copyright © Claire Llewellyn 2001

ISBN 0 7496 3991 1

Dewey Decimal
Classification Number: 676

A CIP catalogue record for this book is
available from the British Library

Series editor: Rosalind Beckman
Series designer: James Evans
Picture research: Sue Mennell
Photography: Steve Shott

Printed in Hong Kong, China

Acknowledgements

Thanks are due to the following for kind permission to
reproduce photographs:

Corbis Images pp. 16t (George McCarthy), 16b (Royal Ontario
Museum), 18b (Kevin Fleming) 22 (Jacqui Hurst)
Robert Harding Picture Library pp. 9b, 17b and back cover
(Wilson North/Int. Stock), 21t
Science Photo Library pp. 18t (Tommaso Guicciardini),
19t (Geof Tompkinson), 23t (Colin Cuthbert)
Still Pictures pp. 17t (Julien Frebet), 19b (Mark Edwards)
Telegraph Colour Library pp. 9t (V.C.L.), 15t (Arthur Tilley),
20 (R. Sacha), 21b (Tom Tracey), 25b (Paul Epley),
26 (David Seed)
Franklin Watts p. 12b (Chris Fairclough)

Thanks are also due to John Lewis for their help with
this book.

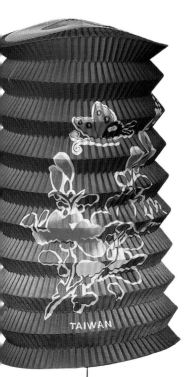

Made of paper

All the things in these pictures are made of paper. Can you name them? What do these things feel like? Do they all feel the same?

Material words

Which of these words describe paper?

cold   thick   shiny

sticky   stretchy

stiff   solid

heavy

soft   strong

dull

hard   warm

hard-wearing

spongy   light

crisp

colourful

rough   smooth

thin

bendy   slimy

springy

runny

squashy

Orange Juice

Take a look

This whole book is made of paper. Look at it carefully. Has it been made from more than one kind of paper? If so, why is that?

Paper is smooth

Most paper has a smooth **surface**. This makes it good for writing or drawing, or for printing on big machines.

Writing on paper

Writing on paper is a way of storing information. We use notebooks, address books and calendars to record all the things we want to remember. Writing on paper is also important in communicating with others. Letters and posters are just two ways of sharing ideas.

Addresses

JANUARY

1	2	3	4	5	6	7
8	9	10	11	12	13	14
15	16	17	18	19	20	21
22	23	24	25	26	27	28
29	30	31				

Drawing on paper

You can draw and paint on paper, and then hang your pictures on the wall. Artists and *designers* use paper to make sketches. This helps them to try out ideas for all the different kinds of things they work on, such as paintings, buildings, furniture and clothes.

A clothes designer at work.

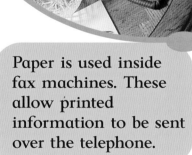

Paper is used inside fax machines. These allow printed information to be sent over the telephone.

Printing on paper

Huge rolls of paper can be put into printing machines to print newspapers, books and magazines.

At home, computers and *faxes* are other machines that print paper.

Fantastic fact

People once wrote by cutting into stone or making marks in clay. It is much easier to write on paper!

9

Paper is strong

Some paper is very strong. It can be used to protect and package many different kinds of goods. Paper is also used to make cardboard, the strongest paper of all.

To Rosalind Beck
66 Green Gardens
London
NW1 8NX

Paper protects

Paper helps to protect things. It can be wrapped or folded around things that might break. A thick layer of tissue paper helps to protect *fragile* glass and china. Padded envelopes help to protect things we send through the post.

A paper package

Many foods are wrapped in paper. It keeps them clean, fresh and dry. A paper package makes a good container for loose foods such as sugar, coffee, rice and pasta. Some foods, such as eggs, need extra protection and are packed in a cardboard box.

Making paper stronger

Cardboard is very strong. It is made from many sheets of paper that have been pressed together. *Corrugated cardboard* is even stronger. It is a strong, spongy material that protects goods from knocks and bumps.

Corrugated cardboard is not smooth; it has dozens of tiny folds. These help to make it stronger.

Fantastic fact

Paper is flexible enough to be folded into different shapes. The art of folding paper is called *origami*. It began in Japan about 1,000 years ago.

Paper is soft

Some paper is so soft that we use it on our skin. Soft paper is also good at soaking up water, and this makes it very useful around the home.

Soft on the skin

Paper that is too soft to be used for writing or packaging can be used to make tissues, toilet paper and table serviettes. All these things can wipe the skin without making it sore.

A paper tissue is soft on your skin, but strong enough for you to blow your nose.

Soaking up water

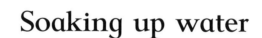

Other kinds of paper are very **absorbent** - they soak up water and other liquids like a sponge. The thick, soft paper used in kitchen rolls is good at mopping up spills. Disposable nappies are made of paper because they need to absorb liquid, too!

Soft but strong

Paper often goes soggy and breaks when it gets wet. Papers that get wet in their normal use are made to be much stronger.

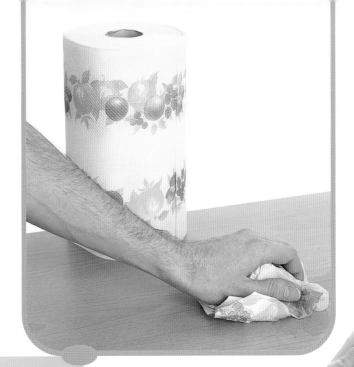

Kitchen paper is strong enough to wipe liquids without tearing.

Teabags and coffee filters are both made of paper and do not break in water.

Try this

Collect a few different kinds of paper and test how absorbent they are. Put a single drop of coloured water or ink on each kind and watch what happens. Does the drop sit on the paper or does the paper absorb it? How far does the colour spread? Write down what you see.

Paper keeps things clean

Paper is used to keep things clean in hospitals, schools and homes. Tablecloths, plates and cups are made of paper because it is clean and safe to use.

At home and school

Sheets of paper are often used to line shelves, cupboards and drawers. Paper provides a clean surface that will not mark dishes or clothes. In school, a layer of newspaper protects desks from paint and glue.

Shelf paper often has a shiny surface so that it can be wiped clean with a damp cloth.

In hospital

Paper is used in hospitals to make doctors' gowns, masks, and simple tools such as **swabs**. Sheets of paper are used on a doctor's couch. All these items are only used once, so patients can be sure they are clean.

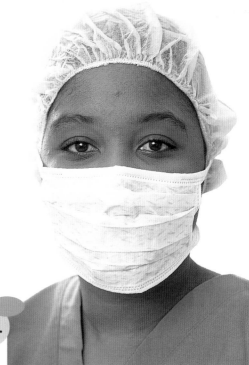

A paper mask and hat help prevent infection.

Eating off paper

On special occasions, such as birthday parties and picnics, we often use paper instead of china or glass. We cover the table with a colourful paper cloth, and eat and drink from paper plates and cups.

Paper goods are clean and colourful. They make a table look very special.

Fantastic fact

Special paper called greaseproof paper is used to line baking tins. It stops cake mixture from sticking to the tins and makes them easier to clean.

Paper is made from trees

Paper comes from natural materials. It is made from the long, stringy threads, called fibres, found in plants. Most of our paper is made from trees.

Wasps buzzing round their papery nest.

Nature's paper

Wasps use paper to build their nests. They make the paper by chewing up tiny bits of wood and mixing it with their **saliva**. The wood becomes a soggy paste that hardens into paper as it dries.

The first paper

People in China began to make paper over 2,000 years ago. They probably got the idea from wasps. The first paper was made from the fibres found in plants, fishing nets and old cotton rags. These materials were pounded into a **pulp**.

The Chinese invented paper. They were the first people to use it for painting.

Today's paper

Most of today's paper is made from wood, which contains very long, thin fibres. A lot of the paper comes from **coniferous** trees, such as fir, spruce and pine. These trees grow quickly and are straight and tall.

Conifers are grown in huge plantations in places like Canada and Scandinavia.

As the trees are harvested, new ones are planted to take their place.

WARNING

Never play with fire. It can be dangerous.

Fantastic fact

Paper is often used to start a bonfire. This is because it burns very easily. After all, it is made from wood!

From logs to pulp

Paper is made from wood pulp, a mixture of mashed-up wood and water. There are different kinds of wood pulp. Each kind of pulp makes a different type of paper.

Wood pulp is made from wood chips mashed with water.

Making the pulp

Huge logs of wood are taken to a **paper mill**. They are chopped into small wooden chips, and mixed with chemicals and water. This makes a soggy mixture known as wood pulp.

At the paper mill, wood chips are stored in piles until they are needed.

Draining the pulp

The pulp is poured into a paper-making machine and spread on to a moving belt. Most of the water drains away through holes in the belt, leaving behind a damp mat made of fibres.

A mat of fibres is left on the belt when the water has drained away.

Some paper is still hand-made. It is popular with artists because it has a special look and feel.

Looking at fibres

Different kinds of wood pulp produce different kinds of paper. Wood pulp made of long fibres makes a good, strong paper. Pulp made of short fibres produces paper of a poorer quality.

Try this

Test the strength of different kinds of paper. How easy are they to tear? Now take a magnifying glass and examine the fibres along the torn edge. Are they long or short? Are they easy to see?

From pulp to paper

The mat of fibres is dried and flattened to make a long sheet of paper. The sheet is rolled up. Then it is either cut into sheets or transported to printers and factories.

Giant rolls of paper at the paper mill.

Drying the fibres

The long mat of fibres is squeezed through rollers and dried in warm ovens. As the fibres dry, they stick together very tightly to make a strong sheet of paper. The paper is smoothed by rollers and wound on to giant rolls.

Using the paper

Some of the rolls of paper are sent to printers to produce newspapers, books and magazines. Some of the rolls are sent to factories, which make paper products such as boxes and other packages. Other rolls of paper are cut into sheets of many different sizes.

Printing machines print on to huge sheets of paper. These are folded and trimmed, and made into newspapers, books and magazines.

These flat packs of cardboard boxes are made from paper.

Fantastic fact

Every minute, a paper-making machine produces a roll of paper over 900 m (990 yd) long and up to 10 m (33 ft) wide. That's enough paper to cover a football pitch!

All sorts of paper

Paper can be treated in many different ways while it is being made.
These different treatments produce coloured, glossy, **waterproof** or other kinds of paper.

Changing the colour

Sometimes different chemicals are added to paper early in its production. If **dye** is added to the wood pulp, it makes paper of a different colour. If glue is added to the pulp, it produces a harder, stronger paper.

Adding a dye to the wood pulp produces coloured paper.

Changing the surface

Some paper treatments happen later in production. Sometimes a special coating is added to the surface. A thin coat of wax or plastic makes the paper waterproof. A coat of starch stops the paper from absorbing liquids such as ink, and makes it suitable for writing on.

Adding a shiny coating to the paper gives it a very smooth feel.

Take a look

Many fine papers and bank notes have a *watermark*. This is made by pressing a wire pattern into the fibres while they are still damp.

Saving paper

In many parts of the world paper is being wasted. More and more trees are being cut down. We need to use paper more carefully by **recycling** it, instead of throwing it away.

Too much paper

Today, people use too much paper. Most of the paper is just used for packaging and ends up as rubbish in the bin. About one-third of all rubbish is made of paper. Throwing paper away is not just a waste in itself. It is also a waste of the trees and **energy** that were used to produce it.

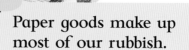

Paper goods make up most of our rubbish.

Reduce, re-use, recycle!

There are three easy ways to save paper. We can *reduce* the amount of paper we use by cutting down on packaging.

A box of chocolates may have more than six layers of paper packaging. But the same chocolates could be bought in one bag.

We can *re-use* many paper products such as old envelopes, boxes and bags. We can *recycle* waste paper by taking it to the paper bank. This paper can be turned into new paper.

Cardboard tubes are dumped before being recycled.

Fantastic fact

About 4,000 trees are used to make just one issue of a daily newspaper.

Recycling paper

The waste paper collected in paper banks is taken to mills for recycling. Recycled paper can be used to make many different things.

A truck stacks paper at a recycling plant. Recycling paper uses less water, less wood, and less energy than making paper from scratch.

At the paper mill

The waste paper is taken to the paper mill where it is shredded into tiny pieces. It is soaked in water and mixed with chemicals to get rid of the ink. This mushy pulp is then added to new wood pulp to make recycled paper.

Recycled paper

The best quality recycled paper is used to make envelopes and writing paper. Poorer quality paper is used to make hand towels, kitchen towels and tissues. Recycled paper is also used to make cardboard to package foods and other goods.

Recycled paper is used for many different things.

Another way of recycling paper is to tear it up and put it in your *compost* heap. Paper rots easily, helping to make compost which is very good for the soil.

Try this

Recycle your greetings cards into attractive gift tags. Take an old card and carefully cut out a round or square tag. Make sure there is no writing on the back! Now punch a hole near the edge of the tag and tie on some ribbon or string.

Glossary

Absorbent   Able to soak up water and other liquids.

Compost   Old fruit and vegetable peelings that are left to rot and then dug into the garden to feed the soil.

Coniferous   Evergreen trees that grow cones and have sharp, narrow leaves that are like needles.

Corrugated cardboard   A kind of cardboard that has many folds to make it stronger.

Designer   A person who makes plans and drawings for products such as furniture and clothes.

Dye   A strongly-coloured substance that is used to add colour to something else such as paper.

Energy   The power that makes machines and living things able to work. We can get energy from fuels, the Sun, water and wind.

Fax machine   A machine that can send exact copies of drawings or documents over the phone.

Fibre	A long, fine thread.
Fragile	Easy to break.
Origami	The Japanese art of folding coloured paper into many different shapes.
Paper mill	A factory where paper is made.
Pulp	The soft, mashed-up wood that has been mixed with water to make paper.
Recycle	To take an object or material and use it to make something else.
Saliva	The liquid inside an animal's mouth that it uses to soften its food.
Surface	The top or outer side.
Swab	A small, soft tool that is used in hospitals to clean a wound or put on a cream.
Watermark	The special mark in a sheet of paper that can be seen when the sheet is held up to the light.
Waterproof	Unable to absorb water.

Index